Walk by Faith

Christian Bible Verse COLORING BOOK FOR Women

Amazing Grace
ACTIVITY BOOKS

Amazing Grace

ACTIVITY BOOKS

Published in 2021 by Amazing Grace Activity Books
www.amazinggraceactivitybooks.com
Copyright © 2021 Amazing Grace Activity Books

This Book Belongs To:

Child of God

Free PDF

AS A SPECIAL THANK YOU FOR GETTING THIS BOOK,
WE WOULD LOVE TO GIVE YOU A FREE GIFT.
GO TO OUR WEBSITE TO GET YOUR
FREE DOWNLOADABLE COLORING PAGES!

www.amazinggraceactivitybooks.com

AND AS YOU COLOR IN YOUR BEAUTIFUL DESIGNS,
DON'T JUST HIDE THEM – GO TO OUR FACEBOOK
GROUP AND SHARE THEM!

www.facebook.com/groups/amzggrace/

"For I know
the plans I have for you,"
declares the Lord,
"plans to prosper you
and not to harm you,
plans to give you
hope and a future."

JEREMIAH 29 : 11

TIP:

THIS COLORING BOOK FEATURES
SINGLE-SIDED COLORING PAGES
TO HELP PREVENT BLEED THROUGH IF USING
MARKERS INSTEAD OF COLORED PENCILS.
AS AN EXTRA MEASURE OF PRECAUTION,
YOU CAN ALSO PUT A SHEET OR TWO
OF PAPER BEHIND THE PAGE YOU ARE
COLORING.

HERE'S HOW TO GET THE MOST OUT OF THIS BOOK:

GET COMFORTABLE.
FIND A CLEAN, QUIET, RELAXING SPACE.
PLAY MUSIC, SPRAY YOUR FAVORITE SCENT,
OR HAVE YOUR FAVORITE SNACK OR BEVERAGE
NEARBY IF YOU WANT TO HELP SET THE TONE.
ORGANIZE YOUR COLORING MATERIALS.
START COLORING AND ENJOY!

THE WORD OF GOD HAS A WAY OF BEING TIMELY AND
FINDING US AT EXACTLY THE RIGHT TIME.
WITH THAT IN MIND, YOU DON'T HAVE TO USE THIS BOOK IN ORDER.
TO HELP YOU MEDITATE ON A PARTICULAR VERSE OF CHOICE,
YOU CAN FLIP THROUGH AND FIND ONE THAT YOU PARTICULARLY
NEED OR THAT PARTICULARLY SPEAKS TO YOU IN THE MOMENT,
AND COLOR IT AS A WAY TO RELAX,
HAVE FUN, AND CONNECT WITH THE WORDS OF GOD
YOU NEED THE MOST AT THE TIME.
HAPPY COLORING!

HOPE THAT IS Seen IS NO Hope at all. Who HOPES for WHAT He can ALREADY See?

ROMANS 8:24

I CAN DO ALL THINGS THROUGH CHRIST WHO STRENGTHENS ME

PHILIPPIANS 4:13

Yet he did not waver through DISBELIEF in the promise of God, but was STRENGTHENED in his faith and GAVE GLORY to God, BEING FULLY PERSUADED THAT GOD was ABLE TO DO WHAT He had PROMISED.

ROMANS 4:20-21

By faith Abraham obeyed when he was called to go out to a place that he was to receive as an inheritance. And he went out, not knowing where he was going.

Hebrews 11:8

THAT your FAITH might NOT REST in The WISDOM OF MEN but in the POWER of God

1 CORINTHIANS 2:5

SHE CONSIDERED HIM FAITHFUL WHO HAD PROMISED

HEBREWS 11:11

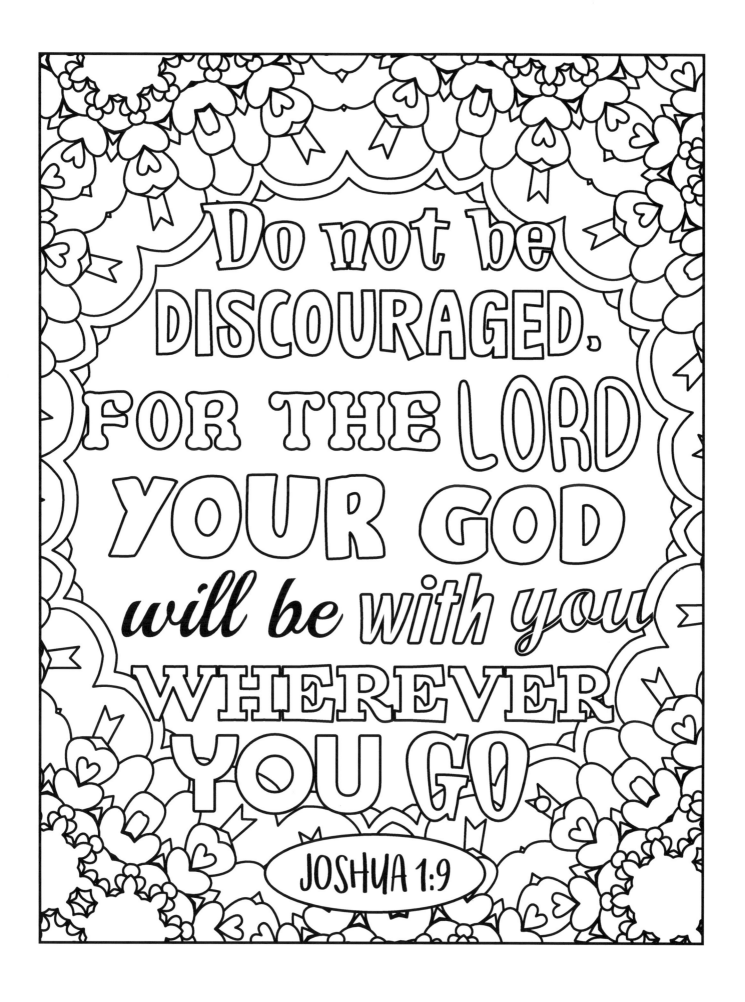

JESUS told him, "Don't be AFRAID; JUST believe."

MARK 5:36

YOU will keep in PERFECT PEACE THOSE WhOSE MINDS are STEADFAST, because THEY TRUST in you.

iSAiAH 26:3

WHAT is seen WAS NOT MADE out of things. THAT Are VISIBLE

HEBREWS 11:3

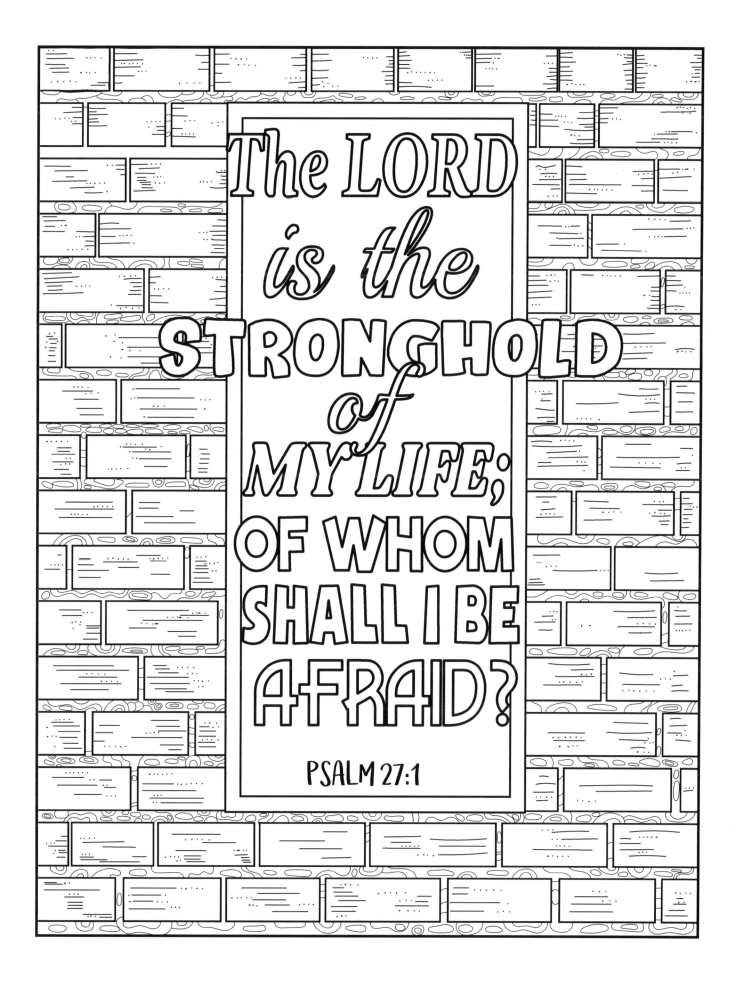

THE LORD is my HELPER; I WILL not be AFRAID.

HEBREWS 13:6

...WHEN HE HAS stood THE TEST HE WILL receive THE CROWN OF LIFE that God has promised TO THOSE who love Him.

JAMES 1:12

CONGRATS, YOU FINISHED!
YOU ARE QUITE THE TALENTED ARTIST.
FEELING PROUD OF YOUR CREATIONS?
SHARE THEM IN OUR FACEBOOK GROUP:
www.facebook.com/groups/amzggrace/

IF YOU ENJOYED USING THIS BOOK
AS MUCH AS WE ENJOYED MAKING IT,
PLEASE LEAVE A REVIEW ON THE PRODUCT PAGE ON AMAZON.

CERTIFICATE
OF COMPLETION

Name: _____

has been recognised as a talented colorist

of coloring books.

Amazing Grace
ACTIVITY BOOKS

Date: _____

HERE ARE JUST A FEW OF
THE OTHER FUN,
FAITH FILLED BOOKS
WE HAVE AVAILABLE ON AMAZON

Made in the USA
Coppell, TX
01 December 2023